3-D WINGS

FABULOUS FLYING MACHINES

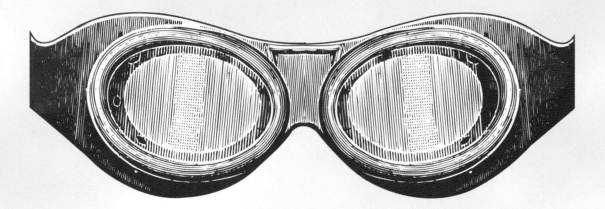

RICK SAMMON

THOMASSON-GRANT

VINTAGE AEROPLANES

Today, people take airplanes for granted.

Jetliners fly high overhead, and we hardly even notice them. They transport us to other parts of the country—and even other parts of the world—in only a few hours.

Single-engine planes are also everyday sightings. These compact machines give "wings" to earthbound creatures who have always dreamed of flight.

Yet less than 100 years ago, there were no planes. The only manned flying objects were hot-air balloons and gliders. The first successful powered flight was made in 1903 at Kitty Hawk, North Carolina, in a wood, wire, and fabric biplane called the Flyer. It was built by two brothers from Ohio, Wilbur and Orville Wright. The historic event lasted only 12 seconds, and the plane travelled only 120 feet—less than half the length of a football field. Later that day, longer flights were made. The longest lasted just under a minute.

Following the Wright brothers' Flyer came other "aeroplanes"—as they were then called (the British still use this spelling)—with one, two, and even three wings. All models had their successes and failures. But the spirit of flying was strong in the hearts of early designers, who often doubled as pilots, and the aviation industry was born.

Our world was changed forever. Eventually, people would be able to visit friends in "no time at all." And in wartime, armies had a new and important weapon.

In this book, you'll get a look at some of the more famous aeroplanes of the World World I era, and some models that became popular in the peacetime years that followed.

When I was photographing these aeroplanes at the Old Rhinebeck Aerodrome in upstate New York, I was taken back to a time of excitement and adventure. It was a time when pilots were dare-devils and heroes, when people marveled at flying altitudes of just a few hundred feet, and when even seeing takeoffs and landings was a thrill.

Imagine yourself alone in the open cockpit of a fighter, being chased by a skillful opponent like Manfred von Richthofen, the Red Baron of Germany. Or picture yourself flying over your own house, doing loops in an antique aeroplane!

Join me now, step back in time, and take an in-depth look at the flying machines of yesteryear.

Rick Sammon, Croton-on-Hudson, NY

BLÉRIOT'S MONOPLANE

In 1903, the Wright brothers made their historic flight in a biplane they built in their bicycle shop. On the other side of the Atlantic Ocean, another self-taught flyer and plane designer, Louis Blériot, was busy at work on a different type of plane—the monoplane.

Blériot made history in 1909 when he crossed the English Channel from France to England in his Blériot XI. The flight took the 36-year-old flyer only 26 minutes, but those few minutes, at an altitude of about 250 feet, paved the way for aircraft of the future.

The monoplane had less drag (wind resistance) than a biplane, so it was often faster than a biplane with an engine of the same size. It also had better visibility. And with one rather than two wings, the monoplane was less expensive to make and easier to transport.

There was one serious shortcoming, however, to monoplanes. With the wooden frames and wire bracing used in early aircraft, the monoplane design was not as strong as the biplane's—some monoplanes had structural failure and broke up in flight!

The Blériot XI—the 11th design of Louis Blériot—had a three-cylinder, 30-horsepower engine. Its average speed was about 40 miles per hour.

"FLYING KITES"

Early aeroplanes had wooden-frame fuselages. The wings were braced with wooden spars. Everything was covered with fabric, and the structure was rigged with tightly strung wires.

These "flying kites," as some people called early planes, look fragile compared to today's metal airliners. However, they were marvels of ingenuity and surprisingly sturdy. Some of the construction techniques were derived from boat building. In fact, early planes were sometimes called "aerial yachts."

At first, aeroplanes flew relatively slowly and at very low altitudes. This 1910 French-designed Hanriot had a top speed of about 50 miles an hour and could fly 1,000 feet off the ground. It was not until 1912 that Jules Vedrines, flying a plane called the Deperdussin Racer, broke the 100-mile-an-hour mark.

Most early planes had wheels, which were needed to gain the necessary speed for takeoff. Some models, including the Hanriot shown here, also had front runners that prevented the plane from tipping over on its nose and crashing during a landing.

Other dangers for early pilots included flying with bad fuel, which was common in the early 1900s, engine overheating, and collapse of the wings.

COMBAT TRAINERS

If you want to fly a plane today, you need extensive training and official certification. You also need lots of practice.

In the early days of flying, young men in their early 20s became pilots in a matter of just a few hours. Understandably, many died tragically trying to become pilots.

One popular World War I trainer in France was this Caudron. It was a single-seater, so there was no one with the would-be pilot to help him correct a potentially deadly mistake. With the early French system of training, a pilot would get intensive training on the ground and then be allowed to practice in a single-seater. This included taxiing up and down the field, making short hops, and finally flying.

This biplane made turns using the rudder and a control feature that actually allowed the rear part of the wing to bend up and down. This is called wing-warping. In modern planes, the same effect is produced by having a hinged surface, called an aileron, at the rear of the wing that can be moved up and down.

WINGS OF WAR

An experienced pilot named Anthony Fokker played an important role in World War I. Although he had no formal training as an engineer, he formed an aircraft company that produced many excellent planes for the Germans, including what was generally considered the best fighter of its time—the Fokker D-VII biplane.

The D-VII was one of the first planes to have a fuselage frame of welded steel tubing. It flew higher and had a better climb rate than most planes of the era.

Late in the war, Fokker produced another very advanced fighter, the Fokker D-VIII monoplane pictured here.

This monoplane was nicknamed the "Flying Razor" by British flyers because when it attacked out of the sun—a technique practiced by skilled combat pilots of the day—its single wing made it almost impossible to see. Highly stream-lined for its time, and equipped with a light and powerful rotary engine, the D-VIII was noted for its speed and excellent climb rate.

The Fokker D-VIII became a model for warplanes of the future, mainly due to the revolutionary design of its wing—which used a stressed-skin form of construction.

GUNS IN THE AIR

Imagine this: you are a pilot in the early days of World War I flying in the 1915 Nieuport 11 pictured here. You see an enemy plane coming straight at you! It's either you or him. So you must attack.

You have to aim your wing-mounted machine gun by actually aiming the aircraft, but you also have to compensate for the way the gun is positioned—far above your line of sight. If the gun jams, you have to loosen your seat belt and stand up in the cockpit to clear it. When you let go of the controls to do this, the plane may go out of control and into a spin!

Similar battle scenes occurred in the early days of the war, and improvements in weapons had to be made.

Eventually, machine guns were mounted on the fuselage, in front of the windshield, allowing for direct sighting and within easy reach of the pilot. One experimental system actually fired bullets *through* the rotating propeller. Special deflector blades made the bullets that hit a blade bounce off, with luck to the side and not at the pilot.

Later, systems were developed that linked the machine gun with the propeller, and the gun only fired when the prop was horizontal and out of the way. Still, misfires could damage the propeller and put the plane or pilot out of action.

A New Kind of War

World War I was the largest and most destructive war the world had ever seen. It was fought mostly in Europe from 1914 to 1918. America entered the war in 1917.

Initially in WWI, the aeroplane was used primarily for observing enemy troops. Later, fighter planes were developed to bring down observation planes. Later still, bombers were used to destroy ground targets.

From the ground, soldiers—like the German on the left and the American on the right in this picture taken at Rhinebeck—fired on enemy planes with rifles, machine guns, and eventually anti-aircraft artillery.

In the early days of the war, when a plane was hit and damaged, the pilot had to try his best to land it—because he didn't have a parachute. Early flyers were not given parachutes for two reasons. One, the equipment was cumbersome and not really perfected. Two, some generals thought that a "safety chute" made a pilot less likely to fight the enemy plane.

FOKKER TRIPLANE

In World War I, a pilot who shot down five or more enemy planes was called an "ace." The most famous ace of all was Manfred von Richthofen, credited with shooting down 80 Allied planes. He was called the Red Baron because he flew a blood-red Fokker DR-I Triplane. The triple-wing Fokker DR-I was fairly slow, but its ability to turn tightly made it a very dangerous adversary.

In three years of combat, the Red Baron brought down more planes than any other pilot, on either side of the war. Pilots who managed to survive a Red Baron attack considered themselves lucky to be alive.

In 1918, the legendary Red Baron was shot down in his DR-I. His enemies buried him with all the honors due a gallant flyer.

OPEN COCKPITS

Before the enclosed cockpits of today's modern airplanes, pilots had to brave the weather in open cockpits.

Just imagine what it was like to fly at a speed of 100 miles an hour or more with the wind driving against your face, on a cold and rainy day. Or how would it feel to fly in an open cockpit at an altitude of 15,000 feet in thin, near-freezing air—without an oxygen mask?

For protection against the elements, pilots had goggles and wore warm, fur-lined leather jackets, pants, gloves, and hats. Because engine oil would often coat the goggles, pilots wore scarves they could use to wipe the goggles clean.

Early planes were not fully equipped with instruments. So, the pilot, especially in bad weather, could not tell where he was going and how high he was flying.

This highly acclaimed Bücker Jungmann biplane was used for training by the Germans in World War II. It had two cockpits. The rear seat was the command seat, complete with basic gauges. The front seat was for a trainee or a passenger.

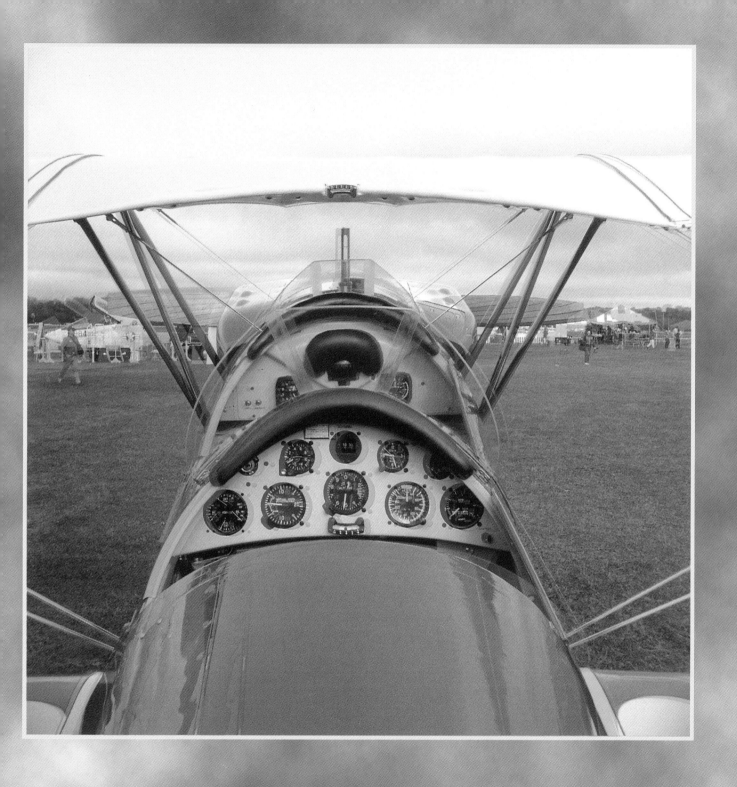

AIR CAMPER

The Pietenpol Air Camper was a noteworthy, "home-built" aeroplane of the early 1930s. It could be made relatively inexpensively because it used a Model "A" Ford engine, which was easy to find and fit into the plane.

This sturdy monoplane was called a camper because it had both a pilot seat and a passenger seat, plus some room for storing camping gear. It could also make easy takeoffs and landings on short, grassy fields.

With only a 40-horsepower engine, the "Camper" had a poor climb rate and was relatively slow. But it was popular with flyers around the country because they could build one and get into the air—not too high and not very far, but into the air nonetheless.

Because the engine was water-cooled, it needed a radiator. Notice where the radiator is placed, right in front of the forward cockpit. The pilot, who sat in the rear cockpit, had to lean to the left or right to see what was ahead.

POWER UP!

The air-cooled radial engine on this 1940s Stearman biplane was considered one of the best engines of the era. The cylinders were arranged in a circle around the crankshaft that turned the propeller. The reliable radial was preceded by a long line of engines of various types, including water-cooled designs dating from the early days of flight.

The Wright brothers designed a water-cooled, gasoline-powered engine built from scratch because they could not find an automobile engine that would fit their plans. But other aeroplane designers used modified car engines with acceptable results.

Light and powerful rotary engines designed specifically for aeroplanes were found on many World War I aircraft. In the rotary engine, the entire crankcase, complete with cylinders, actually rotated around a stationary crankshaft. As the propeller turned, the engine rotated along with it! Planes fitted with rotary engines were difficult to fly due to the gyroscopic effect of the spinning engine.

The first really successful radial engines were built in the 1920s. An efficient radial engine of that period generated about 200 horsepower, which was about 16 times more powerful than the Wright brothers' 12-horsepower engine.

EARLY PROPELLERS

When you look at a plane such as this 1929 New Standard D-25, consider this: each and every part had to be made and tested to specification.

One part, the propeller, as simple as it appears, is a good example of the kinds of challenges designers faced. Wooden props designed for quick takeoffs and fast climbs were not ideal for a fast cruise speed. The opposite was also true. The problem was the "pitch" of the propeller—the angle at which the blade encounters the airflow. To take off quickly and climb well, one pitch angle was required. To get a fast cruising speed, a different pitch angle was needed.

Some early planes were shipped with two propellers, each with a different pitch. This gave the pilot the option to choose the prop that he thought would be best for him.

After World War I, ground-adjustable, aluminium propellers that allowed the pilot to set the pitch before a flight were developed. Finally, in the late 1930s, the pilot was able to adjust the pitch angle of the propeller blade from the cockpit during flight. Pilots would now have more control over the performance of the engine and propeller for better takeoffs, landings, and cruising speeds.

ULTIMATE SPORTS PLANE

In the early 1930s, 15 or 20 Speedwing Travel Air biplanes were built for private pilots who wanted the ultimate sports aircraft. With a sleek design and a 235-horsepower engine, the Speedwing offered great maneuverability—as long as a skilled pilot was at the controls.

The Speedwing also became popular at air shows around the country. Daring pilots raced them at full speed—sometimes upside down—and performed other death-defying stunts.

Some Speedwings were later modified for sky writing and crop dusting. Others became "movie stars" and performed in various films, including "Devil Dogs of the Air," made in 1933 with James Cagney. A Speedwing Travel Air flies in weekend shows at the Old Rhinebeck Aerodrome.